Art Museum

Julie Murray

Abdo Kids Junior
is an Imprint of Abdo Kids
abdobooks.com

Abdo Kids
FIELD TRIPS

abdobooks.com

Published by Abdo Kids, a division of ABDO, P.O. Box 398166, Minneapolis, Minnesota 55439.

Printed in the United States of America, North Mankato, Minnesota.

102019

012020

THIS BOOK CONTAINS RECYCLED MATERIALS

Photo Credits: Alamy, iStock, Shutterstock

Production Contributors: Teddy Borth, Jennie Forsberg, Grace Hansen

Design Contributors: Christina Doffing, Candice Keimig, Dorothy Toth

Library of Congress Control Number: 2019941214

Publisher's Cataloging-in-Publication Data

Names: Murray, Julie, author.

Title: Art museum / by Julie Murray

Description: Minneapolis, Minnesota : Abdo Kids, 2020 | Series: Field trips | Includes online resources and index.

Identifiers: ISBN 9781532188725 (lib. bdg.) | ISBN 9781532189210 (ebook) | ISBN 9781098200190 (Read-to-Me ebook)

Subjects: LCSH: Art museums--Juvenile literature. | Public art galleries--Juvenile literature. | Museums--Juvenile literature. | School field trips--Juvenile literature. |

Classification: DDC 371.384--dc23

Table of Contents

Art Museum

It's field trip day! The class is going to the art **museum**.

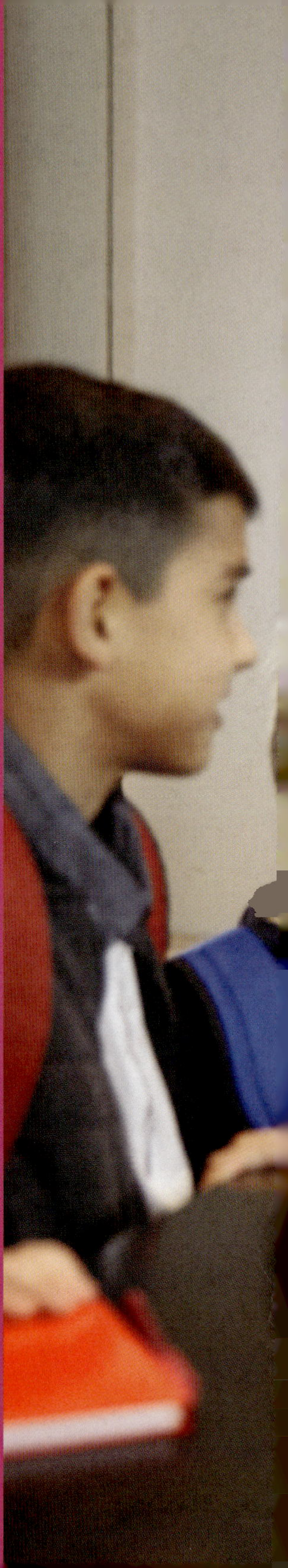

The **guide** walks with the group.

She tells them about the art.

Some of the art is new.

Ben likes all the colors.

Some of the art is old.

Uma looks at the statue.

There are paintings.

Jane likes the flowers.

There is **pottery**. The pot is 5,000 years old!

There is jewelry. Meg looks at the necklace.

There are masks. Tom sees a mask from Sri Lanka.

Have you been to

an art **museum**?

What is at an Art Museum?

masks

paintings

pottery

statues

Glossary

guide
a person who leads others and teaches them.

museum
a building in which objects of interest are stored and shown.

pottery
plates, bowls, pots, and other items made of clay.

Index